Journey Through Space
The Stars

Jeff Wimbush

Crabtree Publishing Company

www.crabtreebooks.com

Author: Jeff Wimbush
Publishing plan research and development:
 Sean Charlebois, Reagan Miller
 Crabtree Publishing Company
Project development: Clarity Content Services
Project management: Clarity Content Services
Editors: Kristi Lindsay, Wendy Scavuzzo
Copy editor: Dimitra Chronopoulos
Proofreader: Kathy Middleton
Design: First Image
Cover design: Samara Parent
Photo research: Linda Tanaka
Production coordinator: Ken Wright
Prepress technician: Ken Wright
Print coordinator: Katherine Berti

Photographs:
Elena Schweitzer/shutterstock: title page;
EpicStockMedia/shutterstock: p4; Natali26/
shutterstock: p5 (top); Elenaphotos21/shutterstock:
p5 (bottom); Markus Gann/shutterstock: p14;
Ingram Publishing/ Thinkstock: p15; Hemera/
Thinkstock: p17; Nelson Marques/shutterstock:
p18; MR LIGHTMAN/ shutterstock: p19; Hemera/
Thinkstock: p20; NASA: p6, 7, 9, 10, 11, 12, 13, 16,
21; Giovanni Benintende/shutterstock: front cover
(stars); © Jaroslaw Wojcik/iStockphoto: front cover
(girls); Thinkstock: back cover

Library and Archives Canada Cataloguing in Publication

Wimbush, Jeff, 1986-
 The stars / Jeff Wimbush.

(Journey through space)
Includes index.
Issued also in electronic format.
ISBN 978-0-7787-5308-7 (bound).--ISBN 978-0-7787-5313-1 (pbk.)

 1. Stars--Juvenile literature. I. Title. II. Series: Journey through
space (St. Catharines, Ont.)

QB801.7.W56 2012   j523.8   C2012-901244-0

Library of Congress Cataloging-in-Publication Data

CIP available at Library of Congress

Crabtree Publishing Company

www.crabtreebooks.com   1-800-387-7650

Printed in the U.S.A./032012/CJ20120215

Published in Canada
Crabtree Publishing
616 Welland Ave.
St. Catharines, Ontario
L2M 5V6

Published in the United States
Crabtree Publishing
PMB 59051
350 Fifth Avenue, 59th Floor
New York, New York 10118

Published in the United Kingdom
Crabtree Publishing
Maritime House
Basin Road North, Hove
BN41 1WR

Published in Australia
Crabtree Publishing
3 Charles Street
Coburg North
VIC 3058

The Stars

Too Many Stars to Count

When you look at the night sky, you can see thousands of tiny dots of light. You cannot count them all. Some stars are so far away, we cannot even see them.

Our Sun is a star. Though the Sun seems huge to us, there are many stars that are larger, brighter, and hotter. Those stars, however, are so far away they seem small. The closest star after our Sun is four **light-years** away. That means the star's light takes four years to get to Earth!

No one is sure how many stars there are. Scientists' best guess is 300 sextillion!

Because the Sun is very close to Earth, it only takes eight minutes for light from the Sun to reach us.

Sun

Earth

What Is a Star?

A star is a giant ball of gases held together by **gravity**. Gravity is the force that pulls objects together. Earth's gravity causes things to fall when you drop them. It also keeps us from floating into space.

A star's gases burn, giving off heat and light. Stars do not burn in the same way a campfire does.

A star's light comes from a process that is more like an explosion!

Stars are **sphere** shapes, just like planets.
A sphere is a shape like a ball.

Star Light, Star Bright

Just like a burner on a stove, the color of a star can tell us how hot it is. The hottest stars are blue. Yellow stars are cooler than blue. Red stars are the coolest. Even the coolest stars are still very hot. The edge of a red star is about 6500 degrees Fahrenheit (3593 degrees Celsius). Stars are hottest in their centers, or **cores**.

Stars can be any size, from small to very large. Stars are grouped based on color, size, and temperature.

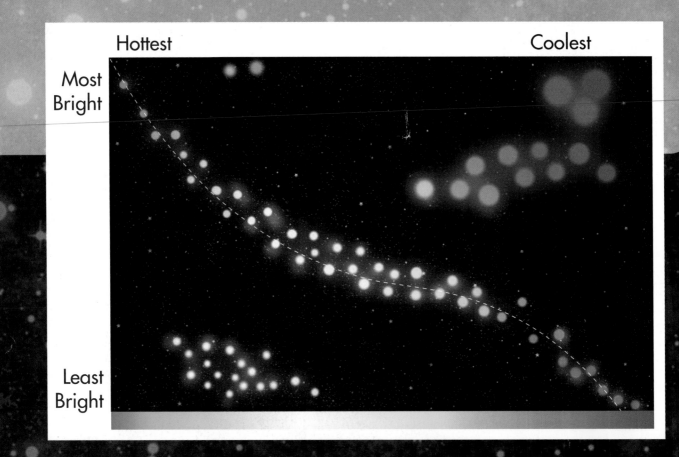

Hottest   Coolest

Most
Bright

Least
Bright

Stars come in many colors and sizes.

The Life of a Star

Stars are born in clouds of dust and gas called **nebulas**. Gravity pulls part of the cloud together into a tight ball. The ball starts spinning and gets so hot that it begins to glow.

The temperature and size of a star changes over time. A star can burn for millions of years or longer. When stars stop burning, they do not go out like a candle. Some stars blow up at the end of their lives. This is called a **supernova**.

This is what a supernova looks like from space.

The colored spot between the stars is a nebula, or a cloud of dust and gas.

Nebula

Clusters and Galaxies

Stars form in groups called **clusters**. Some clusters have hundreds of stars, others have many thousands. Larger groups of stars are called **galaxies**. A galaxy can have trillions of stars! Galaxies and clusters are held together by gravity.

Earth is in the galaxy called the Milky Way. Sometimes when you look up at the night sky you can see the stars grouped together in the Milky Way. They seem so close to each other that they blend together into a long band of light.

Star clusters can be up to 30 light-years across.

Galaxies are huge. They can have many clusters of stars.

Are They Moving?

The stars seem to move across the sky every night. It is not the stars, however, that are moving. It is Earth that **rotates**, or spins, on its **axis**. Earth's axis is an imaginary line that runs through the middle of the planet from its top to its bottom.

Only one star appears to stay in the same place. That star is named Polaris, or the Pole Star, because it is above the North Pole at the tip of the Earth's axis.

From Earth, we see different stars in the sky at different times of the year. This is because Earth **orbits**, or moves around, the Sun. Stars also move through space. They are so far away, however, it is difficult to see them move.

Activity: Follow a Star

What You Will Need
- a night with clear weather
- a pencil and paper

Steps

Step 1: Find a bright star that is low in the sky.

Step 2: Draw a picture of where the star is, using a landmark such as a treetop or the top of a building.

Step 3: Wait an hour or two. Go back to the same spot you were before. Has the star moved?

To track the movement of a star, you have to use a landmark on the ground.

Connect the Dots

In the past, people tried to find patterns in the stars. These patterns are called **constellations**. People from different times and places made up different constellations and gave them names.

Spotting a constellation can be difficult. It is hard to know which stars to connect. Often, it does not really look like a picture, even after you connect the dots!

The stars in constellations might look as though they are the same distance from Earth. They are not. Some stars are much closer to us than others.

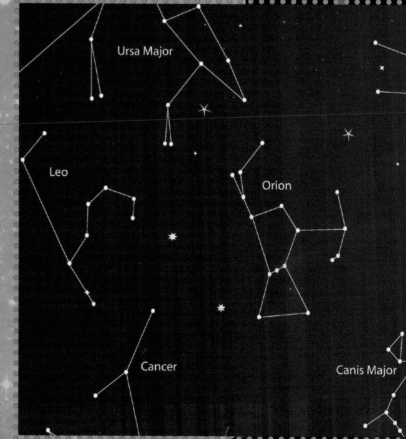

Ursa Major

Leo

Orion

Cancer

Canis Major

ACTIVITY: Find the Big Dipper

What You Will Need
- a clear night
- a compass

Steps

Step 1: Use your compass to find which direction is north.

Step 2: Look into the northern sky. Search for bright stars.

Step 3: Find a line of bright stars with a square shape at one end. Use the photo below as a guide. If you can spot it, you have found the Big Dipper!

The Big Dipper is supposed to look like a giant ladel, or spoon. Once you find the Big Dipper, you can also find Polaris. The bowl of the Big Dipper points toward Polaris.

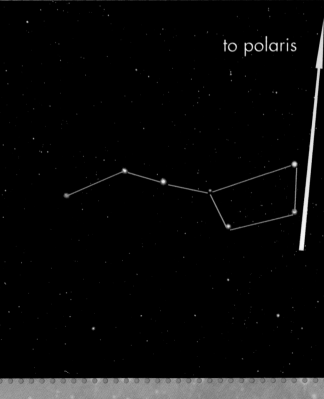

to polaris

Star Watching

The best time to star watch is on a night when the sky is clear. Try to get away from any lights. Lights on the ground can brighten up the sky, just like the Sun does during the day. This can block out your view of starlight.

All you need are your eyes, but a **telescope** can help you see stars much better. This lets you get a closer look at stars. Some stars can only be seen with a telescope.

Safety Rule: Never look at the Sun through a telescope, binoculars, or even with your eyes. Direct sunlight will damage your eyes.

Even when using a telescope, the stars will only appear brighter. They are too far away to view up close.

In case you do not have a telescope,
binoculars can also help you see stars.

Wish Upon a Meteor

Sometimes you can see a light flash across the sky. This is called a shooting star. These are not actually stars, but pieces of rock called meteors. When they enter Earth's atmosphere, they begin to burn up. This gives meteors their bright tails.

Another sky object with a tail is a comet. Comets are big balls of ice that sometimes form a bright tail when they get close enough to the Sun.

A moving light without a tail, it probably a satellite. Satellites are human-made objects that orbit Earth. These objects reflect light and can seem to glow like stars.

Satellites are used for phone or television signals.
Some carry cameras to give us a better view of things
on Earth, such as weather.

Learning More

WEBSITES

www.nasakids.com
Visit NASA Kids' Club for challenging space games and to learn about the latest information about space.

http://starchild.gsfc.nasa.gov/docs/StarChild/StarChild.html
StarChild is a learning center for young astronomers created by NASA, this website offers exciting images and activities.

www.kidsastronomy.com
Kidsastronomy.com is an easy-to-use resource for fun activities and lessons.

http://amazing-space.stsci.edu/gallery/
Visit this gallery to see photos and videos of stars taken by the Hubble Space Telescope.

OTHER BOOKS IN THIS SERIES

The Sun
The Planets
The Moon

Glossary

axis (AK-sihs) An imaginary straight line around which an object spins

constellation (KOHNS-tell-aye-shun) Pattern of stars to which people give meaning

cluster (KLAH-stir) A group of stars held together by gravity; a cluster can range from hundreds to thousands of stars

core (kohr) The innermost layer or center

galaxy (GAL-axe-see) Group of stars, gases, and dust held together by gravity; a galaxy can have trillions of stars

gravity (GRA-vih-tee) The force of attraction between matter

light-year (LITE-yeer) The distance light can travel in a year, or about six trillion miles

nebula (NEB-you-lah) A space cloud of dust and gas that forms stars

orbits (OR-bitz) Travels around another object in a single path in space

rotates To turn about a center point or an axis

sphere (SFEER) A ball-shaped object

supernova (SU-per-no-vah) The explosion of a very large star in which the star temporarily gives off up to one billion times more energy than the Sun

telescope (TEH-leh-skohp) Instrument used to make distant objects appear closer and larger

Index